WILDLIFE IN DANGER

HONOR HEAD

Badger Publishing Limited
Oldmedow Road,
Hardwick Industrial Estate,
King's Lynn PE30 4JJ
Telephone: 01438 791037

www.badgerlearning.co.uk

2 4 6 8 10 9 7 5 3

Wildlife in Danger ISBN 978-1-78464-105-4

Text © Honor Head 2015

Complete work © Badger Publishing Limited 2015

All rights reserved. No part of this publication may be reproduced, stored in any form or by any means mechanical, electronic, recording or otherwise without the prior permission of the publisher.

The right of Honor Head to be identified as author of this work has been asserted by her in accordance with the Copyright, Designs and Patents Act 1988.

Publisher: Susan Ross
Senior Editor: Danny Pearson
Publishing Assistant: Claire Morgan
Designer: Fiona Grant
Series Consultant: Dee Reid

Photos: Cover Image: Frans Lanting/FLPA
Page 4: Image Broker/REX
Page 5: NASA Images
Page 6: © Keren Su/China Span/Alamy
Page 7: © NetPhotos/Alamy
Page 8: © epa european pressphoto agency b.v./Alamy
Page 9: Bruce Adams/Associated Newsp/REX
Page 10: © Frans Lanting Studio/Alamy
Page 11: © Steve Bloom Images/Alamy
Page 12: imageBROKER/REX
Page 14: Image Broker/REX
Page 15: F1 Online/REX
Page 16: © Rolf Nussbaumer Photography/Alamy
Page 18: © Papilio/Alamy
Page 20: Last Refuge/Robert Harding/REX
Page 22: FLPA/REX
Page 24: © LOOK Die Bildagentur der Fotografen GmbH/Alamy
Page 26: © Westend61 GmbH/Alamy
Page 27: Cultura/REX
Page 29: © Sean O'Neill/Alamy

Attempts to contact all copyright holders have been made.
If any omitted would care to contact Badger Learning, we will be happy to make appropriate arrangements.

WILDLIFE IN DANGER

Contents

1. Disappearing animals   5
2. Edge of extinction   8
3. No hiding place   16
4. Empty seas   22
5. Back from the edge   28

Questions   31

Index   32

Badger
LEARNING

Vocabulary

amphibians   poachers
destruction   settlements
endangered   threatened
organisations   traditional

1. DISAPPEARING ANIMALS

We share our planet with some amazing wildlife, such as birds, mammals and insects. But today, many of these wonderful creatures are endangered:

- 25% of all mammal species are endangered
- 12% of birds are endangered
- 33% of the world's amphibians are endangered

Tigers, rhinos, mountain gorillas, giant pandas, Asian elephants and orangutans are all endangered or at a high risk of becoming extinct in the wild. This means that the only place where these animals can be seen is in zoos or wildlife reserves.

Soon, there may be no more tigers hunting in the forests at night, or elephants walking across the African plains, or pandas chewing bamboo in the mountains of China.

Gone forever

The World Wildlife Fund (WWF) is a charity that helps to save wildlife. The WWF estimates that at least 10,000 species become extinct every year.

There are many reasons why species become extinct and most of these are to do with humans. Some of the main reasons are:

- habitat destruction
- pollution of the air and the seas
- illegal hunting
- climate change

WOW! facts
Earth has lost about 50% of its wildlife in the past 40 years.

2. EDGE OF EXTINCTION

In Africa and Asia, the demand for elephant tusks and rhino horns is pushing these animals close to becoming extinct in the wild. Elephant tusks are carved to make ivory jewellery and ornaments. Rhino horn is used in traditional Chinese medicine.

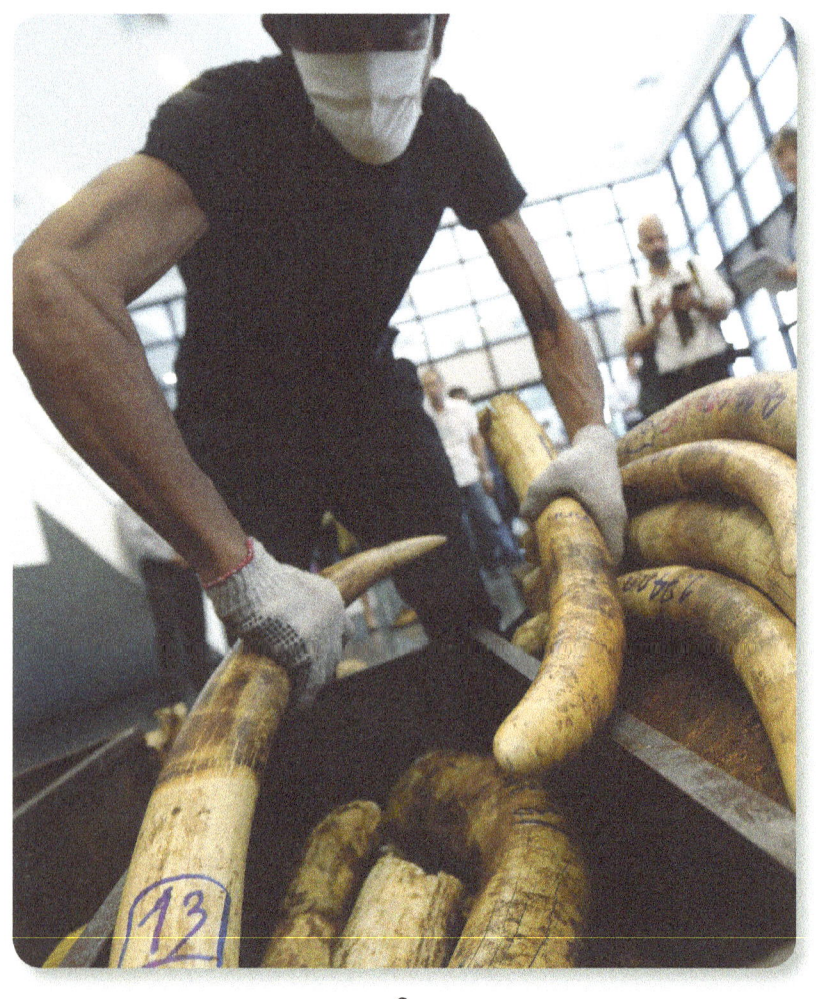

Rhino watch

It is illegal to hunt rhinos and elephants. In wildlife parks in Africa, armed wardens track rhinos to protect them from poachers who kill the rhinos just for their horns. But because rhino horn is worth a lot of money poachers are very clever. They use military-style helicopters, night-vision goggles and guns fitted with silencers to kill the rhinos.

WOW! facts

50,000 elephants were killed illegally in 2013.

Living together

Poaching is not the only problem faced by endangered animals. Different habitats around the world are being destroyed.

Why?
- to create land for farming
- to build roads and houses
- because of climate change

In Africa and Asia, people need land to grow food or to keep cattle. But elephants can trample on crops, kill cattle and damage property. This can lead to human-animal conflict because people kill the animals to protect their land.

Name: African elephant
Found: Mid and South Africa
Habitat: Grasslands and forests
How many left: 600,000
Reason endangered: Killing for ivory, habitat destruction, human-animal conflict

Melting away

Climate change means our world is getting warmer. In the Arctic, the thick sea ice that covers the oceans is melting. As the Arctic ice melts away, the ocean gets bigger. This means there will be more fishing and possibly mining for oil.

This is a real danger for polar bears that live on the sea ice.

Search for food

Polar bears walk across the ice to reach their hunting grounds. As the ice shrinks, it becomes harder for the bears to reach their food. They have to travel further and can become exhausted and starving. Polar bears will hunt closer to human settlements, which will lead to human-animal conflict.

Name: Polar bear
Found: Arctic
Habitat: Sea ice
How many left: 20,000–25,000
Reason endangered: Climate change

Tiger trouble

For hundreds of years, tigers have been hunted for sport. Now there are only around 3000 tigers left in the wild.

Why are tigers hunted?
- for their skin
- for use in medicine
- to keep in zoos and for some people to keep as pets

Tigers are a protected species but poaching has increased as more people want tiger skins and parts of their bodies for medicine.

If poachers kill a female tiger then her cubs will die too. Cubs under two years cannot survive without their mother to help them hunt.

WOW! facts

No two tigers have the same pattern of stripes.

3. NO HIDING PLACE

Disappearing forests

Our planet is covered in huge forests that are home to thousands of species of mammals, birds and insects.

The animals that live in forests need the trees for food and shelter. If the forests disappear so do the animals, especially primates such as monkeys and apes.

Orangutans are the largest mammals that live in trees. In the past 20 years, 80% of the rainforest where they live has been destroyed by illegal logging. That is when trees are cut down to make timber for building homes, furniture and other goods.

Another big threat to orangutans and other wildlife is the destruction of the rainforest to plant trees for palm oil. Palm oil is used to increase the shelf life of goods, so they can be on sale longer in shops and supermarkets.

Name: Orangutan
Found: Sumatra
Habitat: Rainforest
How many left: 7300
Reason endangered: Forest clearance, hunting for meat and pet trade

WOW! facts

Every hour, an area of rainforest the size of 300 football pitches is destroyed for palm oil trees.

Fussy eaters

The killing of giant pandas by poachers is very rare but pandas are still a very endangered species. Why?

Pandas live in the bamboo forests of China and 99% of their diet is bamboo leaves, roots and stems. The human population of China is growing rapidly and huge amounts of bamboo forest have been cleared to make way for housing, farming and for firewood.

Pandas now have less forest to live in and their food supply is decreasing. The government of China is working closely with the WWF to create panda reserves.

Name: Giant panda
Found: China
Habitat: Bamboo forests
How many left: 1600
Reason endangered: Destruction of habitat

Gorilla warfare

Gorillas face many threats from humans:

- Their forest habitat is being destroyed for mining and timber.
- They are hunted for their meat and their babies are taken as pets by local people.
- Human illnesses can be passed onto gorillas and a common cold can wipe out a whole gorilla group.

There have been wars in the part of Africa where gorillas live, and soldiers shoot them to eat or to sell. Wardens trying to protect the gorillas can be threatened or killed by the soldiers.

Name: Mountain gorilla
Found: Uganda, Congo, Rwanda in Africa
Habitat: Tropical forests
How many left: Around 880
Reason endangered: Destruction of habitat, hunting for meat, pet trade

4. EMPTY SEAS

Oceans cover up to 70% of our planet. They are full of creatures from tiny krill to gigantic whales.

How is our ocean wildlife threatened?

- pollution of the oceans
- bad fishing practices – such as over-fishing and dragging huge nets
- whaling – some countries still allow whale-hunting
- climate change

Over-fishing

If too many adult fish are taken out of the ocean, there are not enough left for the population to continue, so the species dies out. This is called over-fishing.

Many countries are now trying to practise safe fishing.

Safe fishing is when fishermen leave enough fish in the sea to make sure the fish population survives.

Tangled in nets

Some fishermen use huge nets, which are dragged along the bottom of the sea.

Hundreds of thousands of marine turtles and more than 300,000 small whales, sharks, dolphins and porpoises are caught in these nets and are killed.

Fishing nets now threaten 26 species of sea bird with extinction. This includes penguins who get caught in the nets.

WOW! facts
Over 100 million sharks are killed each year.

Bloody seas

Some countries are allowed to kill a small number of whales each year but many thousands of whales are killed each year illegally. Whales are hunted for their meat and other body parts.

Shark fin soup is a luxury dish in many Asian countries. Each year thousands of sharks are caught, have their fins cut off, and then are thrown back into the sea to die a slow death.

Name: Great white shark
Habitat: Warm, tropical oceans
How many left: Estimated 3500
Reason endangered: Game fishing, hunting, caught in nets

Sea pollution is another growing problem. Rubbish from ships and the land is filling our seas killing birds, mammals and fish. Birds and other animals eat plastic bags and other rubbish mistaking it for food.

Over one million seabirds die each year from getting tangled up with plastic rubbish, such as netting and the plastic holders used for cans of drink.

WOW! facts

A turtle found dead in Hawaii had over a thousand pieces of plastic in its stomach.

Lost coral

Coral reefs are made up of soft-bodied animals, called polyps, that build a protective shell around themselves. The reefs create a home for other animals, such as fish, crabs and starfish.

What damages coral?

- pollution
- divers
- boat anchors
- fishing (blasting)

Coral is also affected by climate change. Global warming is making the seas warmer and this bleaches the coral so that it turns white. When this happens, it starts to die.

5. BACK FROM THE EDGE

There is a lot that can be done to help save our wildlife in danger. Many charities are working to help protect threatened species.

Victory for Virunga

Virunga National Park in the Congo is the oldest national park in Africa. It is home to elephants, lions, chimps, hippos and a quarter of the world's critically endangered mountain gorillas.

The WWF has recently saved Virunga from oil mining with a massive publicity campaign and a petition.

Thousands of people signed the petition online and now the oil company has agreed to stay away.

Golden success

The golden lion tamarin is one of the smallest monkeys in the world. In the 1980s its numbers fell to just 200 in the wild. This was due to hunting for the pet trade and habitat loss in Brazil.

The WWF launched a conservation programme. Golden lion tamarins were bred in zoos and then released back into the wild. There are now more than 1000 in the wild, but they are not out of danger.

You can help too

Here are a few things you can do to help:

- Buy food that contains only responsibly sourced palm oil.

- Plant wildflowers to help endangered bees and butterflies.

- Don't buy souvenirs made from animals – especially ivory.

- If you snorkel or dive, don't damage the coral by treading on it.

- Wherever you are, always get rid of your rubbish safely. Use a bin or recycle.

- Try going vegetarian once a week. Growing vegetables uses much less land and resources than farming animals does. That means it destroys fewer habitats and helps to slow climate change.

Every little bit we do may help to save another species from becoming extinct.

Questions

According to the WWF, roughly how many species become extinct each year? *(page 7)*

Why are animal habitats being destroyed? *(page 10)*

What is human-animal conflict? *(page 11)*

How are polar bears threatened by climate change? *(page 13)*

What animals are threatened by fishing and why? *(page 24)*

Why do you think it is important to have charities like the WWF?

INDEX

amphibians 4, 5
Arctic 12, 13
bamboo 6, 18, 19
climate change 7, 10, 12,13, 30
crops 11
elephant tusks 8
extinct 6, 7, 8, 30
farming 10, 18, 30
grasslands 11
habitats 10, 30, 31
helicopters 9
illegal 7, 9, 16
illegal logging 16
mammals 5, 16, 26
night-vision goggles 9
orangutans 6, 16, 17
palm oil 17
poaching 10
polar bears 12, 13
primates 16
property 11
rhino horn 8, 9
shelf life 17
silencers 9
tigers 6, 14, 15
World Wildlife Fund (WWF) 7